STEM Projects in **MINECRAFT**

The Unofficial Guide to
Making Maps in
MINECRAFT®

JILL KEPPELER

PowerKiDS
press

New York

Published in 2020 by The Rosen Publishing Group, Inc.
29 East 21st Street, New York, NY 10010

First Edition

Editor: Greg Roza
Book Design: Rachel Rising
Illustrator: Matías Lapegüe

Photo Credits: Cover, 1,3,4,6,8,10,12,14,16,18,20,22,23,24 (background) Evgeniy Dzyuba/Shutterstock.com; pp. 4,6,8,10,12,18 (insert) Levent Konuk/Shutterstock.com; p.5 Dmitry Rukhlenko/Shutterstock.com; p. 7 AridOcean/Shutterstock.com; p. 8 DeawSS/Shutterstock.com: p. 11 Dmitry Natashin/Shutterstock.com; p. 22 Africa Studio/Shutterstock.com.

Cataloging-in-Publication Data

Names: Keppeler, Jill.
Title: The unofficial guide to making maps in Minecraft ® / Jill Keppeler.
Description: New York : PowerKids Press, 2020. | Series: STEM projects in Minecraft | Includes glossary and index.
Identifiers: ISBN 9781725310582 (pbk.) | ISBN 9781725310605 (library bound) | ISBN 9781725310599 (6 pack)
Subjects: LCSH: Map drawing-Juvenile literature. | Minecraft (Game) – Juvenile literature.
Classification: LCC GV1469.M55 K47 2020 | DDC 794.8-dc23

Manufactured in the United States of America

CPSIA Compliance Information: Batch #CWPK20. For Further Information contact Rosen Publishing, New York, New York at 1-800-237-9932.

Contents

Cartography Quest. 4

So Many Maps 6

Starts with Sugar Cane 8

Pixels and Pictures. .10

Zoom Zoom Zoom 12

Copy That 14

Trading Up 16

Buried Treasure 18

Map Wall 20

Making Mods. 22

Glossary 23

Index. 24

Websites. 24

Cartography Quest

Imagine that your family sets off on a trip somewhere new. In the beginning, you'd probably recognize many of the things around you, such as the streets, the buildings, and other landmarks. In time, though, you probably wouldn't know where you were, especially if there were no signs. If you didn't have directions, how would you get home? You'd probably look at a map!

Cartography is the art and science of making maps and charts. You can make maps in the game of *Minecraft*, too. That can keep you from getting lost as you explore the huge game world around you.

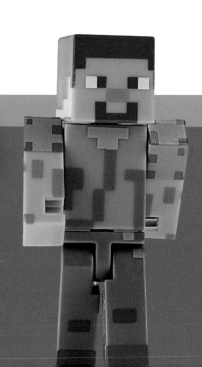

MINECRAFT MANIA

The **default** type of world in some types of *Minecraft* is called an infinite, or never-ending, world. These worlds aren't really infinite, but they can go on for a very long time!

Real-world maps come in many different forms. There are old paper maps that show how much of the world people hadn't explored then... and there are new map apps for smartphones that constantly update where the nearest restaurants are!

So Many Maps

People have been making maps for a very long time. In fact, historians have found maps on clay tablets that are more than 4,000 years old! Maps can show many things—from the streets in your neighborhood to the borders of countries around the world. Some maps show weather systems, currents in the oceans, or the locations of natural **resources**.

Cartography is related to geography, the study of places on Earth. Topography includes the features (such as hills or lakes) in an area of land and refers to the art and science of making maps that show those features.

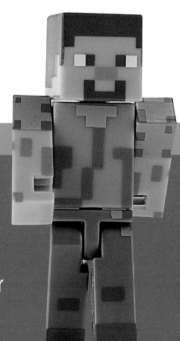

MINECRAFT MANIA

On a *Minecraft* map, you can tell where the waterways are deeper because they'll be a darker blue. Higher elevations mean lighter colors on in-game maps.

Topographic maps may show the **depths** of the oceans and the heights of the mountains in an area. Many use color shading to do this. That's also true in *Minecraft*.

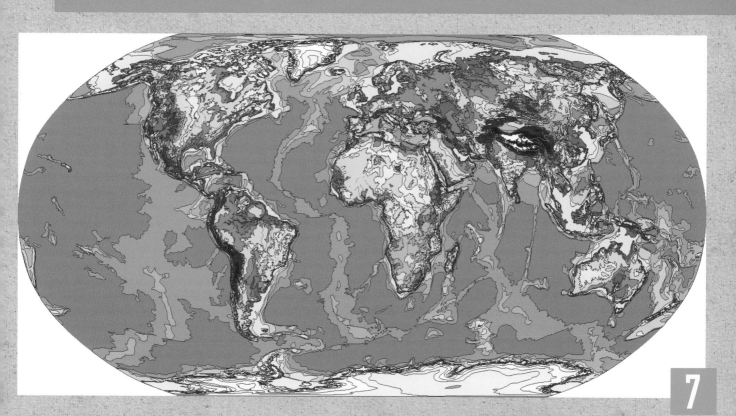

Starts with Sugar Cane

A *Minecraft* map starts with paper, and to make paper, you need sugar cane. These green stalks grow along the water in many *Minecraft* **biomes**. Three pieces of sugar cane will make three pieces of paper.

To make an empty map, you'll need nine pieces of paper. If you want to make a locator map in some games, though, you'll need eight pieces of paper and a compass. You can make a compass with four iron ingots, or bricks, and a piece of redstone dust. This kind of map has a small arrow on it to show you where you are on the map.

sugarcane

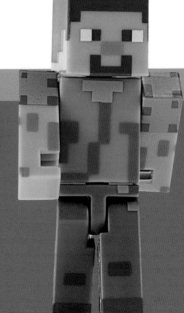

MINECRAFT MANIA

A compass is a tool that's used to find direction. In the real world, it has a needle that always points north. In *Minecraft*, a compass always points back to your **spawn** point.

You can also use *Minecraft* sugar cane to make sugar. In the real world, people use the sugarcane plant to make both paper and sugar, too.

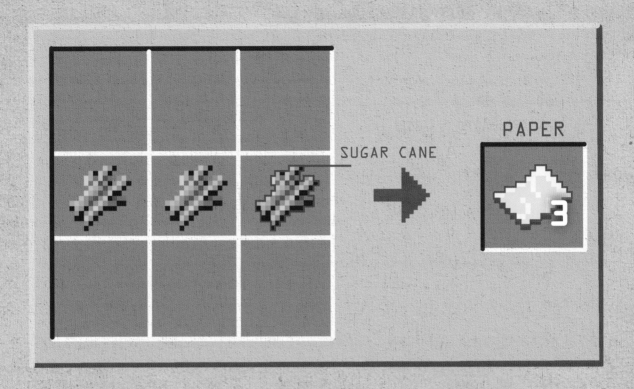

SUGAR CANE

PAPER

3

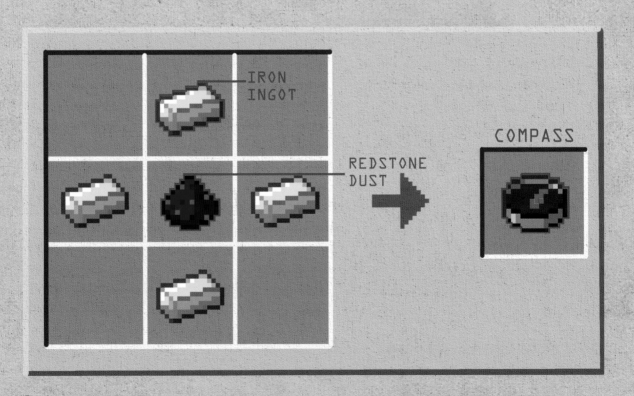

IRON INGOT

REDSTONE DUST

COMPASS

Pixels and Pictures

When you hold a *Minecraft* map that hasn't been activated yet, it's called an empty map. When you activate it, it will start to show the area around you. With a basic level map, this may be a big enough area that the map will already be completely filled in. Maps start at zoom level 0. They show an area of 128 by 128 blocks. Each map **pixel** stands for one block.

This level of map shows the most **detail**, although it doesn't show much area. Every map pixel will show the color of the most common **opaque** block in the area.

MINECRAFT MANIA

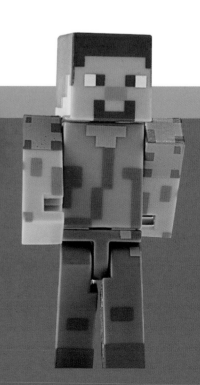

Keep in mind that different types of *Minecraft* work a little differently. Some types have only locator maps. Some show all biomes as the same color. Others have maps only in one zoom level. *Minecraft* often changes, too!

Grass, leaf, and water colors may be different in different *Minecraft* biomes. A map may show that. It will also show snow and sand in frozen or desert biomes.

Zoom Zoom Zoom

While a basic level map doesn't show much, you can zoom your map out in some types of *Minecraft* if you have more paper and an **anvil**. It takes eight more pieces of paper to zoom a map out another level. There are five total map zoom levels, from 0 to 4. A map zoomed out to level

4 shows an area of 2,048 by 2,048 blocks. Each map pixel stands for 16 by 16 blocks. As you move around a *Minecraft* world holding a map, the map will fill in, showing the area around you.

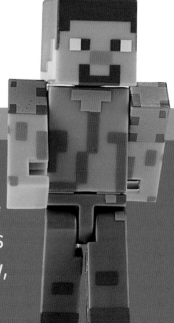

MINECRAFT MANIA

In some newer *Minecraft* **versions**, you may be able to find cartography tables in villages or make your own. You can use these to copy, zoom, or lock maps.

Minecraft maps always **align** to a **grid**. If you move out of the area shown on a certain map, you can start a new map, zoom it to the same level, and fill it in without it overlapping the first map.

ZOOM LEVEL 0

ZOOM LEVEL 1

ZOOM LEVEL 2

ZOOM LEVEL 3

ZOOM LEVEL 4

Copy That

You can also clone, or copy, maps in *Minecraft*. You will need an anvil, a crafting table, or a cartography table depending on which version of the game you're playing. The copy will have the same zoom level as the original. The parts of the original that have been explored and filled out will be copied on the clone.

If you put one copy of a locator map in an item frame, any copies of that map will show a green arrow with the location of the framed map. This can be useful to help you remember where a base or another location is!

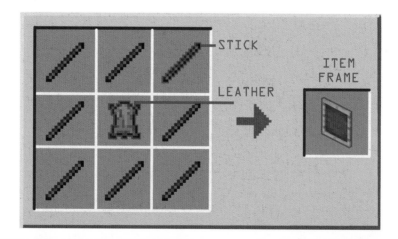

MINECRAFT MANIA

You can make an item frame with a piece of leather and eight sticks and hang it up. You can create framed maps, wall clocks, or other decorations in *Minecraft* with this!

Trading Up

Making maps isn't the only way to get them. Some villages in *Minecraft* have cartographer villagers. They may sell empty maps in exchange for emeralds. Cartographers also sell special explorer maps. Ocean explorer maps guide the player to an ocean monument, and woodland explorer maps guide the player to a woodland **mansion**.

These maps are a lot more expensive, though. They can cost 12 to 28 emeralds (and a compass) each! However, monuments and mansions both have rare loot that you can't find anywhere else in *Minecraft*. You can find them on your own, but it's usually easier with a map.

MINECRAFT MANIA

Explorer maps (which also include buried treasure maps) look different from regular maps. They have the outlines of land and water and a small picture or "X" for the structure in question.

You can only find woodland mansions in dark forest biomes. They're very rare and may be very far away.

Buried Treasure

There's one more type of map in *Minecraft*, but you have to hunt for it! You can find buried treasure maps in some underwater ruins and in shipwrecks. These maps have a red "X" on them. If you travel to the site of the "X" and dig at the middle of it, you'll find a buried treasure chest full of loot. These chests are usually in the middle of sandy beaches. Sometimes, they're underwater.

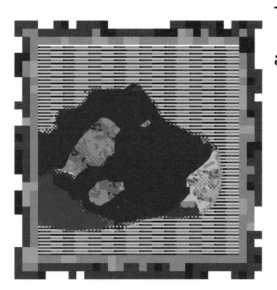

The loot in treasure chests will always include a special item called the heart of the sea. This is the only place you can find that item.

MINECRAFT MANIA

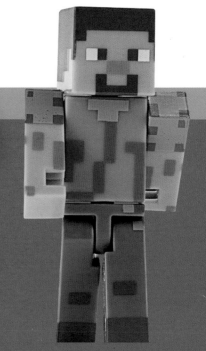

With a heart of the sea and eight nautilus shells, you can make an item called a conduit. When you activate a conduit in a frame of certain blocks underwater, you get special underwater powers.

Map Wall

After you've built a good-sized base in *Minecraft*, you might find you have room for more than one map on your wall. You can hang as many item frames as you want and, if you create and fill in a bunch of non-overlapping maps at the same zoom level, you can make a huge map that covers a lot of your *Minecraft* world.

Map walls look nice, but they can also be useful. They can let you look at an overhead view of your world and help you remember where resources, biomes, and structures are—just like real-life maps.

Think about the math to figure out how much of your *Minecraft* world your map wall covers. If your maps are at the 0 zoom level (128 by 128 blocks) and you have a rectangle made of three maps, how many blocks does your map wall cover?

Making Mods

You can make your *Minecraft* creations even more exciting with modifications, or mods. Using a computer program called ScriptCraft, you can create new blocks, change the way the game functions, and make your own games. Imagine what you could create! You might be able to make maps that you can reset for different events or maps that help you find unusual treasures.

If you're interested in learning how to create mods in *Minecraft*, visit the website below. You'll find the information needed to get started with ScriptCraft and build your own *Minecraft* mods.

https://scriptcraftjs.org/

Glossary

align: To line up together.

anvil: A heavy iron block on which metal is shaped. In *Minecraft*, an item made from 31 pieces of iron and used to change and repair items.

biome: A natural community of plants and animals, such as a forest or desert.

default: Describing something that happens or is done when nothing else is changed.

depth: An area that exists far below a surface.

detail: A small part of something.

grid: A pattern of lines that cross each other to form squares.

mansion: A very large, fine house. In *Minecraft*, a big, three-storied structure with many rooms that sometimes appears in dark forest biomes.

opaque: Not letting light through.

pixel: Any one of the small dots that come together to form a picture on a television or computer screen.

resource: Something that can be used.

spawn: To bring forth. In video games, when characters suddenly appear in a certain place.

version: A form of something that is different from the ones that came before it.

Index

A
anvil, 12, 14

B
biomes, 8, 10, 11, 17, 20
buried treasure, 16, 18, 19

C
cartographer villager, 16
cartography tables, 12, 14
compass, 8, 9, 16

I
item frame, 14, 15, 20

M
mountains, 7

O
ocean, 6, 7, 16
ocean monument, 16

P
paper, 5, 8, 9, 12
pixel, 10, 12

S
shipwreck, 18
spawn point, 8
sugar cane, 8, 9

U
underwater ruins, 18

V
villages, 16

W
woodland mansion, 16, 17

Websites

Due to the changing nature of Internet links, PowerKids Press has developed an online list of websites related to the subject of this book. This site is updated regularly. Please use this link to access the list:
www.powerkidslinks.com/stemmc/maps